Made for you
SUMMER

SEASONAL RECIPES FOR GIFTS
AND CELEBRATIONS

About Sophie

Born and raised in Sydney, now living with her family on their farm just outside Orange in country New South Wales, Sophie Hansen trained in journalism and has over 20 years' experience as a features writer. She has contributed to *Australian Country Style* and *Outback* magazines; she was an editor for Slow Food International's English website, lived in Italy for 3 years and is fluent in Italian. In 2013 she set up her blog, *Local is Lovely*, and her podcast, *My Open Kitchen*, is going into its third season. Sophie has been awarded Australian Rural Woman of the Year in recognition of her commitment to rural communities. She believes in simple, tasty and seasonal food, made with love and shared generously.

Instagram: @locallovely @myopenkitchen

Made for you
SUMMER

SEASONAL RECIPES FOR GIFTS AND CELEBRATIONS

Make ~ Wrap ~ Deliver

Sophie Hansen

murdoch books
Sydney | London

CONTENTS

Food for thought

Is there a better way to show someone that you care than by cooking for them? And not just cooking for them, but also taking the time to wrap and deliver an edible care package to their door? I really don't think so.

This is thoughtfulness on so many levels. And the best part, as they say, is that there can be just as much pleasure in the giving as the receiving of gifts, particularly edible ones! Especially when you double the recipes (highly recommended) and fill your own fridge, cake tins and pantry at the same time.

Made For You: Summer is a collection of recipes that I hope will inspire you to not only cook and share good, simple, seasonal food with your own family, but to make it for others, too – for friends who might be needing a little extra care and love; friends who are grieving, recovering, heartbroken or overwhelmed. And for friends you want to be sure are eating well, or for the kids of your friend who is in hospital so he or she knows that the kids are taking a good muffin or thermos of casserole or bag of biscuits to school with them.

There are bolstering summer buffets of delicious dishes all made in advance, ready to be pulled from the fridge and served up with crusty bread and wine; there are picnic recipes for warm summer days and nights; there are smoothies for kids or friends who need to fill up with goodness but have neither the time or inclination to make them for themselves; there are terrines that will make sandwiches for days and chutneys to have with them, plus jams, morning tea recipes (iced teas and tarts) for office birthday parties or gatherings at home or the park. And there are bolstering recipes for comforting, easy food that

people need when things get bad or just too much. This is simple, seasonal food that says I love you, I made this for you and I'm here for you.

Packing up your care parcels

I think that if you have gone to the effort of making a beautiful cake or casserole, a little bit of effort in making your care parcels look as gorgeous as they're going to taste goes a long way. Why not pick some summer roses and bundle them into a jam jar with a little water in the bottom? Or wrap a warm loaf cake (perhaps the Brown sugar and spice zucchini loaf on page 51) in a pretty tea towel or muslin, then tie it with twine and tuck a few sprigs of rosemary or some flowers under the bow. Having a little basket or box of twine, ribbons, cards and nice pens handy in the kitchen really helps make this happen. And please, don't send off care packages in your very best, most expensive containers or casserole dishes, especially if the recipient is going through a difficult time. You don't want to give them one more job to do (washing and returning your container!). Instead, give food away in boxes, jars, cheap second-hand casserole dishes that you don't mind never seeing again (opportunity shops are great for these) or foil trays.

Practical tips for giving food

Warmer weather does bring a few challenges when it comes to packing up and dropping off edible care packages. The safest thing to do is pack food in an insulated bag or a cool box surrounded by ice bricks and to check that your intended recipient isn't going to be out for the whole day when you are dropping off your package!

Beeswax wraps are eco-friendly, plus they're super cheap and easy to make!

And when preparing food, please always stick to these golden rules of thumb: wash your hands before cooking and be aware of safe temperatures and storage times. Once cooked, cool food on the bench until the steam stops rising, then place it in the fridge – don't let food cool completely on the bench. And don't put hot food straight into the freezer – cool it in the fridge first. Cooked food can generally be safely stored in the fridge for 3 to 4 days only.

To freeze casseroles, divide them into servings of a size that suits your family or the family they are heading to, then place in freezer-safe containers or bags, label with the name of the dish and date, and freeze for 2 to 3 months. Avoid freezer burn by using good thick, resealable bags or quality containers and leave a couple of centimetres at the top of the bag or container to allow the food to expand when frozen. The best and safest place to thaw frozen food is in the fridge.

Watercolour gift tags

One cute way to decorate or style your food gifts is to hand paint a label or tag for them. If I can do it, I promise you can too! I'm no artist, but I can do a simple line drawing of a cherry or an apple or a heart and paint it with forgiving watercolour paint. It makes a super simple but super lovely touch. Add a little wheel of watercolour paints and some pens to your basket of wrapping supplies and they'll always be handy and ready to use.

Beeswax food wraps

These wraps have become popular in recent years as a smart, eco-friendly alternative to plastic wrap. And while you can find them in shops, beeswax wraps are usually fairly expensive. But here's the good news: they're super cheap and easy to make. So grab some fabric (an old shirt or pillowcase) and make up a bunch of wraps to give away as presents and/or wrap gifts, sandwiches for school lunches, cover bowls of leftovers and so on.

You'll need 200 g (7 oz) solid beeswax (find it online or in speciality stores), 1 tablespoon olive oil, pinking shears, an old paintbrush, baking paper, a few baking trays and 6–8 fabric rectangles (they'll need to fit on your baking trays, so use that as a size guide).

Preheat the oven to 150°C (300°F). Line your baking trays with baking paper and place a piece of fabric on each. Melt the beeswax in a glass bowl over a pan of simmering water, stir in the oil, then brush it over the fabric. Pop in the oven for a few minutes, then brush again so the wax evenly and lightly covers the fabric. Hang on a clothesline to dry and they're ready to use. Wash beeswax wraps in lukewarm water, never in the dishwasher! If you find them a bit stiff, just work with your hands for a minute until the warmth makes them pliable.

Italian summer buffet

Vitello tonnato ~ Melon and prosciutto
Amaretti and dark chocolate roasted peaches ~ Cherry frangipane galette

During my late twenties, I called the northwestern Italian province of Piedmont home, and this rather grown-up menu is a catalogue of my Italian favourites from that time. The dishes can all be prepared in advance and served either at room temperature or warmed up, so it can be made ahead and just taken out of the fridge when you're ready. Present it buffet-style, with lots of crusty bread for an excellent Sunday lunch or dinner.

This would also be a great meal to prepare and put in the fridge of a friend who has a large number of people to feed, when it's actually the last thing in the world they feel like doing.

This delicious menu is a catalogue of my Italian favourites.

VITELLO TONNATO

Vitello tonnato can be found on pretty much every osteria menu across Piedmont. It's a classic dish of poached veal knuckle, thinly sliced and served on a bed of rocket (arugula) under a blanket of tonnato sauce, which is essentially a tuna–spiked mayonnaise (it sounds weird but is truly wonderful). I once visited an osteria in the town of Alba and was served a main dish of one onion, slow cooked for hours so it was a globe of caramelised sweetness, doused in tonnato sauce. It was one of the most memorable meals of my life and so inspiring to see the humble onion served as the star of a main course.

You see how awesome and versatile this sauce is? Make a double batch to serve with everything from onions to roasted capsicums (peppers), grain salads or grilled short–loin lamb chops.

One of the best things about this dish is that it can (and actually should) be made up to 2 days in advance, then covered tightly and left in the fridge for the veal to absorb all the flavours of the sauce. Served with crusty bread, it's a complete meal solution done and dusted in advance.

The dish pictured here was made in Tuscany while I was cooking for one of the art classes my mum, Annie Herron, hosted for a few years. I used the classic veal in this case, but at home I give it a more local twist by using a lightly seared fillet of the venison we produce on our farm.

TONNATO SAUCE

½ cup (120 g) home-made or best-quality mayonnaise
185 g (6½ oz) tin tuna in olive oil
4 anchovy fillets, drained
2 Tbsp capers, rinsed
Juice of 1 lemon
2 Tbsp olive oil

Put the mayonnaise, tuna (with the oil from the tin), anchovies, capers, lemon juice and olive oil in the bowl of a food processor or blender and blitz until you have a smooth, thick sauce. Check the flavour and add more lemon juice or salt and pepper to taste.

Store in a jar or covered container in the fridge for up to a week.

VARIATION
Make the tonnato sauce thicker by using a little less mayonnaise and serve it as a dip or spread. It's really yummy spread on sourdough with a slice of tomato and some chilli flakes – something I happen to be eating as I write this and nodding in enthusiasm for its deliciousness!

MELON AND PROSCIUTTO

The combination of cool, sweet rockmelon and salty, chewy prosciutto is an established summer staple in Italy, and perfection on a hot summer day. A plate of this with another of rocket (arugula), a few warm ripe tomatoes, a ball of fresh mozzarella cheese and some good olive oil with a bottle of chilled rosé for lunch is up there with my best meals ever. And it takes all of 5 minutes to throw together. All you do is find a nice firm rockmelon, cut it into wedges, remove the skin and wrap each wedge with a piece of prosciutto. Keep it in the fridge until serving time.

POACHED VEAL

2 Tbsp olive oil
1–1.3 kg (2 lb 4 oz–3 lb) veal nut
1 onion, roughly chopped
2 carrots, roughly chopped
2 celery stalks, roughly chopped
A few cloves, bay leaves and juniper berries
1 cup (250 ml) white wine

Heat the oil in a large flameproof casserole dish over high heat and sear the veal all over for a few minutes on each side. Remove from the pan and set aside.

Add the vegetables and aromatics to the pan and cook over medium heat for 5 minutes. Pour in the wine and let it bubble, stirring often, for a minute or so. Return the veal to the pan and pour in 3 cups (750 ml) water (or enough to just cover the meat). Bring to the boil, then reduce the heat to a simmer. Cook the veal for 15 minutes (it will feel firm but a little springy), then remove it from the liquid and set aside to cool.

The poaching liquid can be turned into a lovely, rich veal stock. To do this, put the pan over high heat until reduced by at least half (it will take about 40 minutes). Strain and store in the fridge or freezer to use in your next casserole, soup or risotto.

TO SERVE

4 handfuls rocket (arugula)
3 lovely, ripe, room-temperature tomatoes, quartered
4 anchovy fillets
1 Tbsp capers, rinsed
1 Tbsp flat-leaf parsley, roughly chopped
Olive oil, for drizzling
2 lemons, quartered
2 baguettes, sliced

Scatter the rocket across a platter, thinly slice the veal and arrange slices on top of the rocket. Spoon the tonnato sauce over the meat so it covers it fairly generously, but leave the edges uncovered. Tuck in the tomato wedges and sprinkle with the anchovies, capers, parsley and a good drizzle of olive oil. Place a few lemon wedges around the edges and serve with crusty bread.

SERVES 6

AMARETTI AND DARK CHOCOLATE ROASTED PEACHES

I absolutely love serving these peaches for dessert with vanilla ice cream or cream, and they're pretty much the only dish I make or take to dinner parties on hot summer nights. One or two chilled peaches with some Greek-style yoghurt also make a fabulous breakfast or brunch.

80 g (2¾ oz) unsalted butter, cut into small cubes, plus extra for greasing
6 ripe yellow peaches
6 amaretti biscuits
½ cup (75 g) finely chopped dark chocolate
¼ cup (45 g) soft brown sugar
1 cup (250 ml) rosé or light white wine

Preheat the oven to 180°C (350°F). Rub a large ovenproof dish with a little butter.

Halve the peaches and remove the stones. Using a small, sharp knife, cut into and around the cavity left by each stone to make it a little bigger. Put the peach halves in the dish, cut side up.

Crush the amaretti biscuits into a small bowl. Mix in the chocolate, butter and brown sugar. Divide the mixture among the peach halves, stuffing as much as possible into each cavity. Drizzle with the wine and bake for 35 minutes or until the peaches are soft but haven't completely collapsed.

SERVES 4–6

These peaches are equally good chilled, at room temperature or served hot straight from the oven.

CHERRY FRANGIPANE GALETTE

Three things I love about this tart: you don't need to blind bake it, it almost looks better if the edges are a bit rough, and it travels beautifully. It's one of my favourites and such a gorgeous way to celebrate the short cherry season. If cherries aren't in season, just use peaches, nectarines, figs or any kind of berry instead. Or if it's coming in to autumn, try using poached quinces.

The pastry can be made in a food processor, but I quite like doing it by hand, feeling the flour and butter coming together and taking the time (no more than 5 minutes) to quietly knead it together. Plus, by the time I get my food processor out, find the blade, lid and so on, then make the pastry, clean said parts and put them away, I don't think there's much time difference between the two processes. And the former is definitely more pleasant than the latter.

Sweet shortcrust pastry
200 g (1⅓ cups) plain flour, plus
   extra for dusting
⅓ cup (40 g) icing sugar
¼ tsp ground cardamom
   (see page 68 for my ground
   toasted cardamom)
A pinch of salt
150 g (5½ oz) chilled unsalted
   butter, cut into small cubes
¼ cup (60 ml) iced water

Frangipane filling
80 g (2¾ oz) butter, softened
½ cup (110 g) caster sugar
¾ cup (80 g) almond meal
1 Tbsp plain flour
1 egg
1 tsp natural vanilla extract

To assemble
3 cups (450 g) pitted cherries
¼ cup (50 g) demerara sugar

To make the pastry, combine the flour, icing sugar, cardamom and salt on a work surface. Bring into a mound and make a well in the centre. Fill the well with the cubed butter and a splash of the iced water. Use the heels of your hands to bring everything together, working the butter into the flour and adding more water as needed. Keep going until you have a rough dough. Shape into a disc, cover with plastic wrap and place in the fridge to rest for 30 minutes.

For the frangipane filling, cream the butter and sugar together until pale and fluffy. Fold in the almond meal, flour, egg and vanilla, mixing until smooth. Keep the frangipane at room temperature if you're using it soon, otherwise place it in the fridge for up to a week, or freeze it.

Preheat the oven to 200°C (400°F). Line a baking tray with baking paper. Lightly dust your work surface with flour, then gently roll out the chilled pastry into a large round, about 3 mm (⅛ inch) thick. Carefully transfer the dough to the tray.

Spread the frangipane mixture over the pastry in a 1.5 cm (⅝ inch) thick layer, leaving a 5 cm (2 inch) border. Arrange the cherries on the frangipane, piling them on top of each other. Bring in the pastry edges, pinching with your fingertips or folding to form little pleats. Sprinkle with the demerara sugar and bake for 25 minutes or until the pastry is golden brown. Serve the galette warm or at room temperature with custard (page 75), ice cream, cream or yoghurt.

NOTE
You may find that the recipe makes more frangipane mixture than you need, but this isn't a bad thing. Roll up any excess in baking paper and freeze it. For a quick dessert, cut some frozen puff pastry into squares, top each with a few slices of frozen frangipane and let it thaw a little. Top with a few slices of peach, a few berries or other seasonal fruit, pinch up the pastry to form an edge and bake until golden.

SERVES 4–6

If I were an organised person,
this menu is what I'd always
pack for long summer car trips.

Playing it cool

Paydirt salad with peaches, tomatoes and mint
Cold soba noodle salad with trout and pickled cucumber ~ Mum's pork and pistachio terrine
Raw chocolate peppermint slice ~ Raw raspberry, orange and cashew slice

If I were an organised person, this is what I'd always pack for long car trips in summer, accompanied by our road trip playlist. I would happily eat the two salads every day of summer. The two slices are nourishing in the sense that they're made from whole, good ingredients that will fill you or your intended recipient with nuts, good fats and good feelings. Even if they're not exactly health food.

PAYDIRT SALAD
WITH PEACHES, TOMATOES AND MINT

Every year, on our way home from holidays, we stop at Paydirt Eatery in Braidwood, New South Wales. This recipe is my interpretation of a lunch I enjoyed there some years ago. I ordered it as a takeaway and it was presented, wrapped in brown paper, with a large purple fig sitting on top. The fig was warm from the sun, freshly picked from the chef's garden. It was such a memorable experience and everything I aim to achieve in my food – generous, thoughtful and tasty, with seasonal produce as the star of the show.

I encourage you to try this bright, crunchy, tangy and sweet summer salad. It's a total winner on its own or served as a side dish to grilled fish or perhaps barbecued chicken thighs marinated first in soy, honey and mirin.

Thank you, Paydirt, for inspiring this, my new favourite salad. It's not quite as good as yours, but it's still pretty delicious.

2 cups (150 g) finely shredded cabbage
2 handfuls mint leaves
1 handful tarragon leaves
1 cup (175 g) chopped cucumber
1 cup (150 g) cherry tomatoes, quartered
3 French shallots, thinly sliced
2 perfectly ripe peaches, thinly sliced
2 Tbsp nigella seeds
1/4 cup (35 g) raw peanuts

Dressing
1/2 cup (125 ml) lime juice
2 Tbsp fish sauce
1 tsp soft brown sugar
1 tsp very finely chopped red chilli, or to taste

Toss together all the salad ingredients.

Mix the dressing ingredients together in a jar, season and adjust to taste. Dress the salad just before serving.

SERVES 4

COLD SOBA NOODLE SALAD WITH
TROUT AND PICKLED CUCUMBER

This is perfect for hot summer days or nights when you can't bear the idea of cooking. The flavours are gentle but delicious and the cold slurp of the slippery soba noodles is highly comforting.

400 g (14 oz) soba noodles
1 handful mint leaves
1 handful Thai (or regular) basil
  leaves
1/2 handful coriander (cilantro)
  leaves
1/2 cup (60 g) finely chopped spring
  onions (scallions)
1/4 cup (40 g) sesame seeds, toasted
1/4 cup (40 g) poppy seeds
300 g (10 1/2 oz) hot-smoked trout

Pickled cucumber
1/2 cup (125 ml) rice wine vinegar
2 Tbsp sugar
1 long telegraph cucumber, thinly
  sliced
Grated zest and juice of 1 lime

Dressing
1/4 cup (60 ml) mirin
1/4 cup (60 ml) soy sauce
1 Tbsp rice wine vinegar
1 Tbsp sesame oil
1 Tbsp grated fresh ginger

For the pickled cucumber, combine the rice wine vinegar and sugar in a small saucepan. Bring to a simmer and cook, whisking a little, until the sugar has dissolved. Pour into a bowl and pop in the fridge. Once the mixture is cool, pour it over the cucumber and add the lime zest and juice. Cover and set aside while you get everything else ready.

Whisk the dressing ingredients together, then set aside.

Cook the noodles according to the packet instructions. Drain, then rinse under cold water, working the noodles between your fingers to wash away excess starch. Toss the noodles with the dressing.

When ready to assemble, toss the pickled cucumber, herbs, spring onion and seeds through the noodles. Flake the trout over the salad, give a gentle toss and serve, or return to the fridge until needed.

SERVES 4

MUM'S PORK AND PISTACHIO TERRINE

1 handful sage leaves
1 handful flat-leaf parsley leaves
2 garlic cloves
$^1/_2$ tsp sea salt
6 black peppercorns
300 g (10$^1/_2$ oz) pork mince (see Note)
300 g (10$^1/_2$ oz) beef mince
$^1/_2$ cup (70 g) pistachios
$^1/_4$ cup (60 ml) white wine
1 brown onion, finely diced
2 Tbsp olive oil
10 rashers streaky bacon

My mum is a big terrine maker. Her standard picnic basket includes one just like this, along with a bowl of hard-boiled eggs, a loaf of bread, a jar of home-made chutney and some greens.

If you're considering making up a basket of goodies for a family in need of easy meals for tricky days, a terrine is a winner. It can sit in the fridge ready to make into a quick lunch or dinner with a salad, or cut into thick slices for sandwiches, with some chutney.

Combine the sage, parsley, garlic, salt and peppercorns on a chopping board and chop together until fine. In a large bowl, combine the pork and beef mince, the pistachios, wine and herby garlic mixture. Mix together well, then cover and place in the fridge for 1 hour for the flavours to combine.

Meanwhile, put the onion in a frying pan with the olive oil. Cook over medium heat for about 10 minutes or until the onion is completely soft and translucent. Spread out on a tray to cool completely.

Preheat the oven to 160°C (320°F). Line a 30 x 8 cm (12 x 3$^1/_4$ inch) loaf tin with the bacon, placing three strips lengthways along the bottom of the tin and the rest crossways, letting the ends hang over the sides.

Mix the cooled onion into the pork mixture, then press it into the tin. Fold the bacon over the top to make a lid and wrap tightly in foil. Line a roasting tin with a tea towel and place the terrine in the middle (the tea towel stops the terrine from moving around while you're moving the tin in and out of the oven). Place the roasting tin on the middle rack of your oven and carefully pour enough boiling water into the tin so that it reaches about halfway up the sides of the loaf tin.

Bake for 1$^1/_2$ hours, then remove the roasting tin from the oven and let the terrine cool for about 15 minutes in the water bath.

Remove the terrine from the roasting tin. Cover with a sheet of baking paper and weigh down with a few tins of tomatoes or such. Leave the terrine in the fridge overnight or for at least 6 hours. Store in the fridge for 3–4 days.

NOTE
If possible, ask your butcher to roughly mince pork shoulder and a beef chuck cut. Otherwise, regular mince is fine.

SERVES 8–10

RAW CHOCOLATE PEPPERMINT SLICE

The key to this easy slice is the peppermint oil. If you can lay your hands on a proper peppermint essential oil, it will lift the game considerably and transform this into a cooling, completely delightful treat. You should be able to find it at health food shops or online. I have a small bottle that cost me about $40, which I know sounds like a lot but it lasts for ages as you only need a drop or two.

Base
1 cup (160 g) almonds
1 cup (90 g) desiccated coconut
1/3 cup (40 g) unsweetened dark cocoa powder
3 Tbsp rapadura sugar, honey or maple syrup
A pinch of sea salt

Middle
3 cups (270 g) desiccated coconut
1 Tbsp coconut oil
2 Tbsp honey or maple syrup
2 drops peppermint essential oil

Top
1/2 cup (55 g) unsweetened dark cocoa powder
1/3 cup (80 ml) melted coconut oil
2 Tbsp rapadura sugar, honey or maple syrup

Grease and line a 20 cm (8 inch) square cake tin with baking paper. Mix all the base ingredients in a food processor until well combined. Press into the tin and pop in the freezer for 20 minutes.

For the middle layer, clean out the food processor, then add all the ingredients and blitz until well combined. Press the mixture over the base, then return to the freezer to set for another 20 minutes.

For the top layer, mix the ingredients in a small bowl until well combined. Pour over the middle layer and smooth the top. Place in the fridge to set for at least 30 minutes, then cut the slice into squares to serve.

MAKES 18 PIECES

RAW RASPBERRY, ORANGE AND CASHEW SLICE

A pretty and super-delicious slice, this makes a great present and is very easy to put together. Keep it in the freezer and transport in a cool box or chiller bag with an ice pack or it will soften and lose shape. As with the peppermint slice, this is a filling treat, so serve in small squares.

Base
1 1/2 cups (225 g) pitted dates
1/2 cup (110 g) 'no-sugar' crystallised ginger
3 cups (480 g) almonds
1/2 cup (125 g) coconut oil
1/2 tsp sea salt

Middle and top
4 1/2 cups (700 g) raw cashews, soaked overnight
 in cold water
1 cup (250 g) coconut cream
1/2 cup (175 g) honey
Grated zest and juice of 1 orange
1 tsp vanilla bean paste
1 drop orange essential oil (optional)
2 cups (250 g) raspberries, plus an extra handful
Dried rose petals, to garnish (optional)

Line a 20 cm (8 inch) square spring-form cake tin with baking paper. Mix all the base ingredients in a food processor until smooth; stop and scrape down the side every now and then. Press into the tin and pop in the freezer for 20 minutes.

For the middle and top layers, clean out the food processor, then tip in the drained cashews, coconut cream and honey. Blitz until smooth. Add the orange zest, orange juice, vanilla and orange oil, if using. Spoon half of the mixture over the base and return to the freezer for another 20 minutes.

Combine the raspberries and remaining cashew mixture and blitz until smooth. Spread over the middle layer. Top with the extra raspberries, then return to the freezer for at least 4 hours before cutting. Store in the freezer, allowing it to soften a little before serving with rose petals, if using.

MAKES 12–18 PIECES

You can use fresh or frozen raspberries for this slice.

Smoothies forever

*Mango, chia, yoghurt and cardamom smoothie ~ Mint, cucumber, spinach and pineapple smoothie
Blueberry, walnut, banana and ginger smoothie ~ Coconut rough smoothie*

Smoothies are excellent to make and give to anyone, especially new mums or friends
with tender tummies, low energy and/or zero time and energy to shop for and prepare
healthy food. A good smoothie repertoire is also handy for school holidays when the kids
are too busy racing to the beach, pool, bike track, wherever, to wait for a proper breakfast.
I reason that if they've put away one big smoothie, loaded with goodness and flavour,
then they have something healthy in their tummies and I haven't completely
dropped the ball.

If you make up a few different smoothies, then even when there's nothing else
in the fridge you can still get some goodness into your day via a quick smoothie hit,
filling and full of condensed energy. When I was pregnant with our first child and
feeling nauseous ALL THE TIME, a cold mango smoothie at 4pm was a major
highlight of my day. My niece Grace named the Coconut rough smoothie and
she's spot on: the rich cacao and coconut flavours will appeal to any sweet tooth
and stop any chocolate cravings in their tracks.

SMOOTHIE NOTES

Dairy-based smoothies should be consumed the day they are made; non-dairy smoothies are fine for up to 2 days but will separate so need a good shake before drinking.

Always keep your smoothies cool. When transporting, please do so in a cool box or chiller bag with a few frozen bricks. And as usual when dropping off food that needs to be kept chilled, try to ensure that your lucky recipients are going to be home or home soon. If it's the latter, leave the box or bag beside the door or in a shady spot and come and pick it up again later.

Another option with these smoothies is to make up 'freezer bags' for you and your friends to tip into a blender with ice cubes and whizz up at will. Fruits such as bananas, mangoes, strawberries, raspberries and pineapple freeze well and make smoothies creamier and colder when whizzed up. Just keep things like soft herbs, greens and cucumbers separate as they don't love a freezer so much.

All four of these recipes make one or two serves. Simply combine all of the ingredients in a high-powered blender and whizz until smooth.

MANGO, CHIA, YOGHURT AND CARDAMOM SMOOTHIE

1 cup (185 g) chopped mango (about 1 mango)
1 Tbsp white chia seeds
¼ cup (70 g) plain yoghurt
1 cup (250 ml) milk
A pinch of ground toasted cardamom (page 68)
4 ice cubes

MINT, CUCUMBER, SPINACH AND PINEAPPLE SMOOTHIE

½ cucumber, roughly chopped
1 handful baby English spinach
1 cup (160 g) roughly chopped pineapple
A few mint leaves
1 cup (250 ml) water or coconut water
Juice of ½ lime
4 ice cubes

BLUEBERRY, WALNUT, BANANA AND GINGER SMOOTHIE

1 cup (155 g) fresh or frozen blueberries
1 banana (preferably frozen)
10 walnuts
1 Tbsp coconut oil
3 cm (1¼ inch) piece ginger
1 cup (250 ml) water
4 ice cubes

COCONUT ROUGH SMOOTHIE

1 Tbsp raw cacao powder
¼ cup (40 g) almonds
¼ cup (20 g) shredded coconut
3 dates, pitted
1 Tbsp chia seeds
A pinch of sea salt
1 cup (250 ml) milk (dairy, nut or coconut)
4 ice cubes

This is a great way to quickly get some goodness into the day.

Catering for a crowd

Glazed ham ~ Jansson's temptation ~ Spiced cauliflower and chickpea salad
Will's crunchy wild rice and currant salad ~ Meringues ~ Poached apricots with ice cream

While this menu is, for my family at least, firmly anchored in Christmas, it would be just as welcome at any big gathering where bolstering food is called for: a 21st birthday, street party, wake, thank you party for staff, community group or local volunteer firefighters.

I know I'm not reinventing the wheel but sometimes it's nice to be reminded how good the simple classics are. They're classics for a reason, and if you feel you need to jazz things up a bit, get creative with the side salads. The two suggested here are my brothers' creations and are firm family favourites.

Big gatherings of any kind can bring their own spectrum of anxiety, so don't let food be one of them. Prepare this menu, delegate a few side dishes and then relax in the knowledge that your efforts will be universally appreciated.

GLAZED HAM

There are many good flavour combinations and options for glazing a ham; this one is my favourite. The inevitable leftovers will provide fillings for sandwiches, substance for frittatas and a tasty option to toss through pasta.

1 whole ham leg, around 6 kg (13 1/2 lb)

Glaze
1/2 cup (125 ml) pomegranate molasses
Juice of 1 lime
Juice of 2 oranges
1/2 cup (175 g) honey
1/4 cup (45 g) soft brown sugar

Combine all the glaze ingredients in a small saucepan. Cook over medium heat, stirring often, for 10 minutes or until you have a lovely glossy glaze.

Preheat the oven to 180°C (350°F). Use a sharp knife to cut around the ham shank, running the knife under the skin and right around the edge of the ham. Gently pull the skin back in one piece, using your fingers to push between the rind and fat. Reserve the skin for storing the ham. Score the fat in a diamond pattern. Cover the shank with foil.

Grab the biggest roasting tin you have and pour in water to come 1–2 cm (1/2–3/4 inch) up the sides. Put a wire rack in the tin, pop the ham on top and brush with a third of the glaze. Place in the oven for 1 hour, pulling the ham out every 20 minutes to baste with the glaze and add more water if needed. Serve warm or at room temperature.

NOTE
Cooked ham must be stored in the fridge. Cover it with the skin you peeled off earlier, then place it in a fabric bag soaked in a vinegar solution (add a good splash of vinegar into a sink a third full of water, then dunk the bag in and give it a good hand wash). You can use a specific ham bag or a pillow case. Rinse and re-soak the ham bag in a vinegar solution every 3 days. Keep the ham for up to a week, but use your common sense – if it smells dodgy, it probably is.

SERVES 10–15

JANSSON'S TEMPTATION

I don't think we've ever had a Christmas when a potato bake of some kind wasn't on the table. If you don't think anchovies will fly at your place, then leave them out, but I find they 'melt' into the dish so beautifully, nobody notices them but they all appreciate the deep saltiness.

35 g (1 1/4 oz) butter, cut into cubes, plus extra for greasing
8 anchovy fillets (or to taste!), plus oil from the jar
1 brown onion, thinly sliced
200 ml (7 fl oz) single (pure) cream
1/2 cup (125 ml) milk
A good pinch of salt
A good pinch of freshly ground black pepper
1 kg (2 lb 4 oz) potatoes (Dutch cream are great for this), peeled and thinly sliced
1 cup (60 g) fresh breadcrumbs (ideally made from sourdough or a nice wholemeal or seeded bread)

Preheat the oven to 200°C (400°F). Brush a large ovenproof dish with butter.

Pour the oil from the anchovies into a frying pan over medium–low heat and add the onion and anchovies, breaking up the latter with a wooden spoon. Cook for about 5 minutes, stirring often.

Combine the cream, milk, salt and pepper in a saucepan and heat just to boiling point. Add the potato and simmer for about 15 minutes or until just tender when pierced with a sharp knife.

Carefully transfer half of the potato mixture to the ovenproof dish. Top with half of the onion mixture, then repeat with the remaining potato and onion mixtures. Sprinkle with the breadcrumbs and dot with the butter. Bake for 35 minutes or until the breadcrumbs are golden and crunchy. Serve warm or at room temperature.

SERVES 6–8

SPICED CAULIFLOWER AND CHICKPEA SALAD

This salad is great to take to a barbecue, picnic or other feast if you're asked to bring a plate – it's good served cold or at room temperature.

1 tsp ground coriander
1/2 tsp ground cumin
1/2 tsp ground turmeric
1/2 tsp chilli flakes (to taste)
1 tsp caster sugar
1/2 tsp sea salt
1 cauliflower, cut into florets
1/3 cup (80 ml) olive oil
2 brown onions, thinly sliced
3/4 cup (150 g) dried chickpeas, soaked overnight
    in cold water, then cooked until tender, or
    400 g (14 oz) tin chickpeas, rinsed and drained
1 handful coriander (cilantro) leaves
1 handful flat-leaf parsley leaves
2 handfuls mixed salad leaves
Juice of 1 lemon

Preheat the oven to 200°C (400°F). Combine all of the spices, sugar and salt in a small bowl. Place the cauliflower on a baking tray. Drizzle with a little of the olive oil, sprinkle with the spice mix and rub to combine. Roast the cauliflower for 35 minutes or until it's beginning to char on the edges.

Meanwhile, heat the remaining olive oil in a frying pan over medium–low heat and cook the onion for 15 minutes or until caramelised.

In a large serving bowl, toss together the cauliflower, chickpeas and onion. Just before serving, add the herbs and salad leaves, drizzle with the lemon juice and season to taste.

SERVES 6 (AS A SIDE SALAD)

WILL'S CRUNCHY WILD RICE AND CURRANT SALAD

Another good option to prepare ahead and transport, this salad is also substantial enough to serve on its own.

1/3 cup (65 g) wild rice
1 1/2 cups (300 g) basmati rice
1/3 cup (80 ml) olive oil
2 red onions, finely diced
1/2 cup (75 g) sunflower seeds
1/2 cup (75 g) pepitas (pumpkin seeds)
1/4 cup (40 g) sesame seeds
1 tsp cumin seeds
1 cup (140 g) dried or fresh currants
1 handful mint leaves
1 handful flat-leaf parsley
2 handfuls baby English spinach

Dressing
1/4 cup (60 ml) olive oil
2 tsp dijon mustard
2 Tbsp red wine vinegar

Put the wild rice in a small saucepan and cover with cold water. Bring to the boil, then reduce the heat and simmer for about 35 minutes or until tender (you may need to top up the water during this time). Rinse and drain, then set aside.

Meanwhile, cook the basmati rice according to the packet instructions (I use the absorption method).

Heat 2 tablespoons of the olive oil in a frying pan over medium–low heat. Cook the onion for 15 minutes or until caramelised. Transfer to a plate.

Wipe the frying pan clean and then return to the heat. Cook the sunflower seeds, pepitas, sesame seeds and cumin seeds until toasted and just beginning to pop.

Combine the rices in a large bowl. Add the onion, toasted seeds, currants, mint, parsley and spinach.

Shake the dressing ingredients in a jar until combined. Pour over the salad and toss, then season to taste.

SERVES 6 (AS A SIDE SALAD)

MERINGUES

My paternal grandmother, Mary, made the world's best meringues – crunchy on the outside and chewy inside. After Sunday lunch she'd put a big plate of them on the table with a bowl of whipped cream and a bowl of passionfruit pulp. We'd sandwich two meringues together with that tangy cream mixture and they were everything. Here they are with poached apricots and ice cream.

Meringues can be a bit tricky to master, I know. The main thing really is getting the measure of your oven and not burning them or turning them brown. My advice is to always err on the side of a lower oven temperature and longer cooking time, rather than rushing and burning them.

3 egg whites
A pinch of salt
¾ cup (165 g) caster sugar

Preheat the oven to 130°C (250°F). Line two large baking trays with baking paper.

Place the egg whites and salt in the bowl of an electric mixer. Whisk until soft peaks form, then begin adding the sugar, 1 tablespoon at a time. Keep mixing for 6 minutes or until glossy and stiff.

Using two tablespoons, make mounds of the meringue mixture on the baking trays, leaving about 5 cm (2 inches) between them. Bake for 45 minutes, then turn off the oven and leave inside to cool.

VARIATIONS
Crush the meringues and serve with whipped cream, a fresh apricot purée and berries (Eton mess at its best).

Make the meringues as discs, top with a little whipped cream and perch half a poached peach, pear or quince on top. Sprinkle with praline and maybe a cloud of Persian fairy floss.

Serve as a pavlova, topped with whipped cream, passionfruit and berries.

MAKES 15–20

My grandmother made the world's best meringues – crunchy on the outside and chewy inside.

POACHED APRICOTS WITH ICE CREAM

Cut 1 kg (2 lb 4 oz) apricots in half, discarding the stones. Combine 1/2 cup (110 g) caster sugar, 1/2 cup (125 ml) wine and 1 tsp vanilla bean paste in a large saucepan and bring to the boil. Add the apricots, then reduce the heat to a low simmer and cover the mixture with a piece of baking paper. Cook for 5 minutes or until the apricots are soft, then remove from the heat. Store in the fridge.

To make the ice cream, churn 1 quantity custard (page 75) in an ice cream machine. Alternatively, freeze the mixture for 1 hour, then whisk until smooth. Repeat the freezing and whisking three times; this breaks up the ice crystals so you have a lovely smooth ice cream. Serves 4–6

Always waiting for special occasions to
do special things lets too many days
pass by without particular note.

Morning tea in the orchard

Fig and peach custard tarts ~ Vanilla, peach and mint iced tea

'How we spend our days is, of course, how we spend our lives.' I love this line from Annie Dillard's book, *The Writing Life*. And it reminds me that always waiting for special occasions to do special things lets too many days pass without particular note.

A morning tea for your co-workers, a welcome to the area present for new neighbours, a birthday morning tea for a friend and so on; these occasions can be elevated to memorable moments thanks to someone going to the moderate effort of buying or making a nice cake or tart, producing a tablecloth and mixing a jug of iced mint tea.

Cue this late summer spread, orchard optional – all you need is a nature strip, a kitchen bench, an office board room, wherever... venue isn't key, but the sentiment is.

FIG AND PEACH CUSTARD TARTS

This blueprint custard tart recipe is an absolute winner, and to make it even easier, you could just buy a ready-rolled sheet of shortcrust pastry or even a frozen tart shell. Then whisk together the custard filling, top with fruit and it's ready to go.

The tart is good either warm or at room temperature. Store it in the fridge for up to 2 days, then gently reheat before serving.

Sweet shortcrust pastry

1 1/3 cups (200 g) plain flour, plus extra for dusting
A pinch of salt
1/3 cup (40 g) icing sugar
150 g (5 1/2 oz) chilled unsalted butter, cut into small cubes
1/4 cup (60 ml) chilled water

Custard filling

1 cup (250 ml) single (pure) cream
2 eggs
1/4 cup (55 g) caster sugar
1 vanilla bean
4 figs, peaches or nectarines, or 1 cup (150 g) berries or poached fruit (quinces would be beautiful)

To make the pastry, combine the flour, salt and icing sugar on a work surface. Bring into a small mound and make a well in the centre. Fill the well with the cubed butter and a splash of the chilled water. Use the heels of your hands to bring everything together, working the butter into the flour and adding more water as needed. Keep working and smooshing with the heels of your hands until you have a rough dough. Shape into a disc, cover and place in the fridge to rest for 30 minutes.

Lightly dust your work surface with flour, then gently roll out the pastry into a large round, about 3 mm (1/8 inch) thick. Gently drape it over the rolling pin and unroll it into a loose-based fluted tart tin, about 23 cm (9 inches) wide and 3 cm (1 1/4 inches) deep. Press the pastry down into the crease where the base meets the side. Roll the rolling pin over the top of the tin, cutting away the excess pastry to create a nice neat edge. Return to the fridge for 30 minutes before blind baking.

Preheat the oven to 200°C (400°F). Prick the base of the pastry a few times with a fork. Line with baking paper and fill with pastry weights, uncooked rice or dried beans. Blind bake for 10 minutes, then remove the weights and baking paper and bake for a further 10 minutes or until the pastry looks pale and dry.

Meanwhile, make the custard filling. Combine the cream, eggs and sugar in a bowl. Using a small sharp knife, cut the vanilla bean in half lengthways, scrape out the seeds, add them to the cream mixture and whisk together. Set aside while you slice the fruit.

Pour the custard into the tart shell and top with the fruit. Bake for 20–25 minutes or until the custard is just turning golden.

MAKES ONE 23 CM (9 INCH) TART

VANILLA, PEACH AND MINT ICED TEA

A jug of this refreshing iced tea goes beautifully with either of the custard tarts on page 40 and it makes a welcome change from the usual hot morning cuppa. It's also a lovely treat to make up and give someone, and will keep in the fridge for a couple of days. Serve it over plenty of ice.

$^1/_3$ cup (30 g) green tea leaves or 6 green tea bags
1 Tbsp roughly chopped fresh ginger
6 cups (1.5 litres) boiling water
2 peaches or nectarines, sliced
1 handful mint leaves
Ice, to serve

Vanilla syrup
1 cup (220 g) sugar
1 vanilla bean, split lengthways

To make the vanilla syrup, put the sugar in a small saucepan with 2 cups (500 ml) water. Scrape the vanilla seeds into the pan and add the vanilla bean. Heat until the sugar dissolves.

Combine the tea, ginger and boiling water in a large heatproof jug and leave to brew for 5 minutes. Discard the tea leaves or bags, pour in 2 cups (500 ml) of the vanilla syrup and the vanilla bean, then transfer to the fridge to cool.

When ready to serve, check the flavour – is it too strong, too sweet or not sweet enough? Add more water or vanilla syrup to taste. Transfer to a large serving jug and add the sliced fruit, mint leaves and ice.

MAKES ABOUT 8 CUPS (2 LITRES)

I like to have a jug of this ready and waiting in the fridge during summer.

Holiday baking

Brunekager ~ Sweet and salty trail mix ~ Cinnamon twists

Summer holidays are the perfect opportunity to fill the kitchen with kids, get the tunes cranking and bake up a batch of cheer. This baking party is a craft and cooking activity rolled into one. Everyone can help, whether it's cutting out biscuits, braiding dough wreaths or measuring and packaging trail mix for outdoor adventures. You might even get some offers to help with the washing up and taste your home-made goodies.

BRUNEKAGER

My family's version of these gently spiced Danish 'brown biscuits' are my favourite. They're wonderful for cutting into shapes or making into classic thin rounds. They last for ages and make the kitchen smell nice and homely. You'll also find these crumbled into Cold vanilla and buttermilk soup (page 71) and are lovely tucked into a basket of goodies.

2 cups (300 g) plain flour, plus extra for dusting
1/2 tsp bicarbonate of soda
2 tsp ground ginger
1 tsp ground cinnamon
1/2 tsp ground toasted cardamom (page 68)
A good grinding of black pepper
A pinch of salt
3/4 cup (165 g) firmly packed soft brown sugar
125 g (41/2 oz) chilled butter, cut into cubes
1/4 cup (90 g) honey
2 Tbsp boiling water

Preheat the oven to 180°C (350°F). Line two large baking trays with baking paper.

Combine the flour, bicarbonate of soda, spices, salt, brown sugar and butter in the bowl of your food processor and blitz until the mixture resembles fine breadcrumbs.

Whisk the honey and boiling water in a small jug. Pour into the food processor and blitz again for a few seconds. Turn the mixture out onto a work surface and bring together into a disc. Wrap in plastic wrap and place in the fridge to chill for 30 minutes.

Turn the dough out onto a lightly floured surface and divide it into three pieces. Roll out each piece of dough to about 3 mm (1/8 inch) thick. This is the fun part – get out your cookie cutters and cut shapes from the dough. Transfer to the trays and bake for 10–12 minutes or until golden. Let the biscuits cool on wire racks, then ice or decorate them as you like.

VARIATION
These are great in ice cream sandwiches. Cut the biscuits into rounds using an 8–10 cm (31/4–4 inch) cookie cutter or glass. Buy or make a nice vanilla ice cream, allow it to soften a little and then spread it out on a shallow baking tray. Return the ice cream to the freezer to firm up a little, then cut it into circles using the same cutter as before. Return to the freezer again to firm up, then sandwich each ice cream round between two biscuits. Keep in the freezer until ready to serve.

MAKES ABOUT 30

SWEET AND SALTY TRAIL MIX

Trail mix is great for car trips, work snacks and, of course, as sustenance when out trail walking. Combine 1 cup (160 g) oven-roasted almonds, 1 cup (45 g) pretzels, 1/2 cup (75 g) pepitas (pumpkin seeds), 1/2 cup (110 g) crystallised ginger, 1/2 cup (75 g) dried cranberries and 1 cup (140 g) roughly chopped white chocolate.

CINNAMON TWISTS

Working with buttery, yeasted, sweet dough is my happy place. I often make different versions of this recipe, from the individual wreaths here to a large one filled with blood orange curd. Don't be put off by the yeast or by the technique – they are both easy to handle and the result is far more impressive than it is difficult. The braiding might take a little bit of practice, but even if it isn't perfect, it will still be delicious!

1 quantity basic sweet dough (page 74)
Icing sugar, for dusting

Filling
100 g (3¹/₂ oz) butter, softened
¹/₂ cup (110 g) firmly packed soft brown sugar
1 tsp ground cinnamon
¹/₄ tsp freshly grated nutmeg

Preheat the oven to 180°C (350°F). Line two large baking trays with baking paper.

To make the filling, mix the soft butter, sugar and spices together.

Turn the dough out onto a lightly floured work surface and gently cut it into six even pieces. Roll out one piece of dough until you have a rectangle about 30 x 20 cm (12 x 8 inches). Spread the dough with one-sixth of the filling. Gently, but as tightly as you can, roll the dough from the longest edge into a long sausage. Use a serrated knife to slice the dough in half lengthways to make two long half-cylinders. Put the halves next to each other, cut sides up, and braid together, forming a wreath as you go. It sounds a bit tricky but really it's not – just press the ends together and place one piece of dough over the other, always with the cut side facing up, then lay the other piece over the top and so on, working it into a circular wreath shape. Press the ends together.

Repeat with the remaining dough and filling, then gently transfer the wreaths to the trays. Bake for about 25 minutes or until the wreaths are risen and golden. Dust with icing sugar and serve warm. If you're serving these the next day, warm them up in the oven.

MAKES 6

Summer care package

Honey-soy chicken legs ~ Spinach and ham tart ~ Brown sugar and spice zucchini loaf

As I write this, in February 2018, a bushfire is burning a few kilometres from our farm. My husband, Tim, is out there with our local Rural Fire Services brigade, along with over a hundred more volunteers on the ground. In the sky is the enormous Nancy Bird, a VLAT (acronym for the somewhat unimaginative name of this fire retardant dropping/life saving Very Large Air Tanker), plus a Hercules plane and a number of helicopters dropping water and working hard to hold containment lines. It's a scary roller-coaster for the rest of us; one minute I look out of the window and think it's all going to be fine, the next it feels as if the billowing smoke is within arm's reach. So with sprinklers on the roof, water pumps and generators at the ready, I sit and wait. While, in the kitchen, batches of biscuits, curry and quiche are working their way through the oven, ready to be dropped off at the control centre to help sustain the wonderful people protecting our houses and livelihoods.

At times like this, people want simple food. Food that their kids will eat too, that can be eaten as it is or needs just a quick burst in the microwave or on the stovetop. Because when people are stressed, hungry, tired and sick of toasted sandwiches, a delivery of simple, ready-to-eat, comforting family food can be a godsend.

HONEY-SOY CHICKEN LEGS

I know I'm re-inventing the wheel here, but these are always such a hit with adults and kids alike that I thought it was worth including them. Mum often made these and I thought they were the most exotic, delicious meal ever. I make them for my kids to the same enthusiastic reception.

8 chicken legs
1/2 cup (125 ml) soy sauce
2/3 cup (235 g) honey
2 garlic cloves, finely chopped
6 cm (2 1/2 inch) piece ginger, finely chopped
Sesame seeds, for sprinkling

Put the chicken legs in a large non-reactive bowl. Whisk together the soy sauce, honey, garlic and ginger. Pour the marinade over the chicken legs and toss well. Cover and place in the fridge for a few hours or overnight.

Preheat the oven to 200°C (400°F). Remove the chicken legs from the marinade and place on a foil-lined baking tray. Sprinkle with sesame seeds and bake for 35 minutes or until the chicken is cooked through – pierce the fleshy part of one leg and check carefully for 'done-ness'. Serve either hot or from the fridge (they're really good cold).

MAKES 8

SPINACH AND HAM TART

This tart transports well and is lovely at room temperature or straight from the oven. It's also a great way to use up left-over Glazed ham (page 34).

1 quantity rough puff pastry (page 74)
2 eggs
1/2 cup (125 ml) single (pure) cream
1/2 cup (50 g) finely grated parmesan cheese
Grated zest of 1 lemon
1 cup (150 g) roughly chopped, thick-sliced ham
1/2 cup (100 g) blanched, finely chopped
  English spinach

Roll out the pastry on a lightly floured surface until about 5 mm (1/4 inch) thick. Drape the pastry over the rolling pin and unroll it into a loose-based fluted tart tin – mine is 20 cm (8 inches) wide and 3 cm (1 1/4 inches) deep. The pastry will shrink back into the tin when cooking, so minimise this by leaving extra at the top and really pushing the pastry down and into each indent in the side of the tin. Trim the edge, leaving about 5 mm (1/4 inch) extra. Return to the fridge for 30 minutes.

Preheat the oven to 200°C (400°F). Prick the pastry base with the tines of a fork. Line with baking paper and fill the base with pastry weights, uncooked rice or dried beans (this stops the base rising during baking). Bake for 10 minutes, then gently remove the weights and baking paper and cook for another 5–10 minutes or until the pastry is just lightly golden and looks dry. Meanwhile, prepare the tart filling.

Whisk together the eggs and cream. Season to taste, then add half of the parmesan and the lemon zest. Pour into the pastry and add the ham and chopped spinach. Sprinkle with the remaining parmesan and some black pepper. Bake for 25–30 minutes or until the top is golden and just firm to touch.

SERVES 6–8

BROWN SUGAR AND SPICE ZUCCHINI LOAF

A good zucchini loaf recipe is handy in late summer when every gardener seems to be swimming in zucchini and bringing bags of them to work in an effort to offload their bounty. Here's my favourite way to make good use of this generous vegetable. Slice and package the loaf to serve fresh, or toast it and top it with a dollop of my Home-made crème fraîche (page 68).

500 g (1 lb 2 oz) zucchini
(courgettes), grated (about
3 large zucchini)
1/4 cup (55 g) caster sugar
1 2/3 cups (250 g) wholemeal plain
flour
2 tsp baking powder
2 tsp ground ginger
1/2 tsp ground nutmeg
1/2 tsp ground cinnamon
A pinch of freshly ground black
pepper
A pinch of salt
1 cup (220 g) firmly packed soft
brown sugar
3 large eggs
1 cup (250 ml) extra virgin olive oil
1 tsp vanilla bean paste

Preheat the oven to 180°C (350°F). Grease and line one large loaf tin – mine is rather long, about 28 x 13 cm (11 1/4 x 5 inches) – or two smaller ones with baking paper.

In a small bowl, mix the zucchini with half of the caster sugar. Place the mixture in a colander over the same bowl and weigh it down with a plate and a tin of tomatoes or similar and leave for at least 10 minutes so as much liquid drains away as possible.

Whisk the flour, baking powder, spices and salt in a large bowl. In a separate bowl, combine the remaining caster sugar with the brown sugar, eggs, olive oil and vanilla, whisking until all the ingredients are really well combined. Gently fold the wet and dry ingredients together. Squeeze any excess liquid out of the zucchini, then fold the zucchini into the batter.

Pour the batter into the tin, smooth the top and bake for 1 hour or until the loaf is beginning to pull away from the sides of the tin and a skewer inserted into the centre comes out clean. Leave in the tin for 5 minutes before turning it out onto a wire rack to cool.

SERVES 8

Summer fruit harvest

Cherry and rose petal jam ~ Apricot and vanilla jam ~ Bottled fruit ~ Fruit cobbler
Stone fruit and redcurrant chutney ~ Raspberry vinegar cordial

When I moved to northern Italy in my late twenties, the first couple of months were dreadfully lonely. I didn't know a soul and I didn't speak Italian – two major road blocks when it came to making friends. I'd catch the train to Turin every Saturday and wander around the outdoor food market. There I dreamt of buying the enormous bunches of mint, asparagus, artichokes and tomatoes to prepare feasts for my friends, before remembering I didn't have any (cue violins). Instead I'd buy bags of strawberries, and spend Sunday making jam. The familiar ritual and smells made my dark apartment feel homely for a few hours at least.

My Italian slowly improved, and I kept taking my work colleagues jars of jam. Gradually they began to involve me in their family outings, drinks, dinners and Sunday picnics. Soon I had a life that was exciting and romantic enough to keep me there – for three years. It turned out to be a wonderful experience, but even now the smell of strawberry jam pulls the shutters of loneliness down fast.

All of this is to say that I will never write a strawberry jam recipe. EVER. I will, instead, offer you these gems: cherry and rose petal, and apricot and vanilla. And because there's nothing as satisfying as putting away a glut of seasonal produce for the lean winter and early spring months, I've included my method for bottling fruit and a few other favourite fruit recipes.

There are few things as satisfying as putting away a glut of seasonal produce.

NOTES ON JAM MAKING

~ The faster jam is made, the fresher and fruitier it tastes, which is why it's best to make small batches of jam – it's easier to cook faster in small quantities.

~ Slightly underripe fruit is best to use in jam, because it will have more acidity.

~ Use a pan with a wide base so that the fruit cooks more evenly and, again, faster.

~ Sterilise the jars before you start – I wash mine well in a hot dishwasher, then heat them in a 180°C (350°F) oven for 15 minutes.

~ You can tie up the lemon pips in a piece of muslin if you want to remove them before bottling. Don't leave them out entirely, as they add lots of good natural pectin that helps the jam set.

~ When jars and bottles are sterilised properly, the preserves reach setting point before bottling, and they are stored in a cool, dark place, jams should have a shelf life of at least 9–12 months, and cordials of 6 weeks. If you're in any doubt at all, store them in the fridge.

CHERRY AND ROSE PETAL JAM

1 kg (2 lb 4 oz) sugar
1 tsp pectin (see Note)
1 kg (2 lb 4 oz) ripe cherries
2 lemons
2 handfuls unsprayed rose petals

Put a couple of small plates in the freezer. Pour the sugar into a large bowl and add the pectin, whisking so it's well distributed.

Now get started on pitting the cherries. (I splurged a few years ago and bought a $20 cherry pitter. It comes into its own every December and I highly recommend any cherry lovers buy one – you'll thank me!)

Place the pitted cherries in a large saucepan and pour in the sugar. Cut the lemons in half and squeeze in the juice and pips, then gently stir to combine. If you have a sugar thermometer, attach it to the side of the pan.

Bring the mixture to a slow simmer. Once the sugar has melted, bring to a rolling boil. Cook, stirring every now and then so the jam doesn't catch or burn on the bottom, for 10 minutes or until the temperature reaches jam setting point – 105°C (221°F). If you don't have a sugar thermometer, do the 'plate test': after about 10 minutes, drop a teaspoon of the jam onto one of the plates you put in the freezer, wait for about 10 seconds, then push your finger through the middle of the jam. If it wrinkles and resists a little then it has reached setting point. If the jam is still runny, cook it for another 5–10 minutes before testing again.

Remove from the heat and stir in the rose petals. Ladle the jam into sterilised jars, filling each right to the top. Screw on the lids tightly and invert the jars onto a board covered with a tea towel (inverting the jars helps create a seal).

NOTE
Adding pectin is optional, but with low-pectin fruits like cherries (and strawberries, blueberries, peaches, pears, figs, etc.), I usually just throw in a little extra so I don't end up with a syrup rather than a jam. You can find pectin in most supermarkets or online via preserving websites.

MAKES ABOUT 3 JARS

I once spent a few freezing days in Venice right before Christmas. One of my main motivations for the trip was to visit the Monastero di San Lazzaro degli Armeni, an Armenian monastery that sits on a tiny island. Its scholarly monks are known for the rose petal jam they make on the island, and the idea of this confection and its creators had captivated me. I'll never forget sitting in the chapel on that bone-chillingly cold day, the pews giving off a hint of the rose oil that's regularly rubbed into them, and feeling overwhelmed by the place and the disappointing fact that they were out of jam.

This is my ode to that moment. I made my rose petal jam on a bright, sunny day in my neighbour's kitchen 16 years later, with her happy babies playing at our feet, the cricket on the radio and my own family just down the road.

This lovely jam is a firm favourite of mine. It makes enough to fill about 8 medium-sized jam jars, but this depends, of course, on the size of the jars you use.

APRICOT AND VANILLA JAM

3.5 kg (7 lb 14 oz) apricots
2 vanilla beans, split lengthways
1 lemon
2.5 kg (5 lb 8 oz) sugar

Place a couple of small plates in the freezer. Preheat the oven to 160°C (320°F).

Cut the apricots in half, removing and reserving the stones. Cut each apricot half into quarters and place in a large heavy-based saucepan or stockpot.

Crack 15 of the apricot stones to reveal the almond-shaped kernel inside. Place these in a shallow dish and cover with boiling water for 5 minutes, then drain and roughly chop (make sure there aren't any hard pieces of shell in there). Add to the saucepan with the apricots.

Scrape the vanilla seeds into the saucepan and add the vanilla beans. Pour in ½ cup (125 ml) water. Cut the lemon in half and squeeze in the juice and pips, then add the lemon halves.

Bring to the boil, stirring often so that nothing sticks to the bottom of the pan and burns. Boil for 10 minutes, at which point the apricots will be lovely and soft. Meanwhile, tip the sugar into a large stainless-steel bowl or baking tray and place it in the oven to warm up – about 6 minutes will do the trick.

After the fruit has been cooking for 10 minutes, pour in the hot sugar. If you have a sugar thermometer, attach it to the side of the pan and cook the jam over high heat, stirring often, for 15 minutes or until the temperature reaches jam setting point – 105°C (221°F). If you don't have a thermometer, do the 'plate test': after 15 minutes, dollop a teaspoon of the jam onto one of the plates you put in the freezer, wait for about 10 seconds, then push your finger through the middle of the jam. If the jam wrinkles and resists a little then it has reached setting point. If it is still runny, cook it for another 5–10 minutes before testing again. Discard the lemon halves.

Ladle the jam into sterilised jars, filling each right to the top. Screw on the lids tightly and invert the jars onto a board covered with a tea towel (inverting the jars helps create a seal).

NOTE
The faster the jam is made, the better it tastes, which is why you warm the sugar before adding it to the fruit. If you added all that cold sugar it would slow down the cooking process.

MAKES ABOUT 8 JARS

I can't imagine a more delicious combination of apricots and vanilla.

BOTTLED FRUIT

Also known as heat preserving, bottling is a fantastic way to preserve seasonal produce. It means that in deepest winter, when the fruit bowl is empty, you can reach into the pantry for a jar of bright and sunny preserved apricots to spoon over your porridge. And in other good news, the whole process – while it can be a touch hot, sticky and time consuming – is as easy as the pie you can make later with your bottled fruit! I don't recommend bottling fruit when you are rushed in any way, so invite some friends over and make an afternoon of it. Set up afternoon tea, play some great tunes and have a good chat while you chop, wash and pack fruit into jars.

THE BASIC BOTTLING RECIPE

Make up a light sugar syrup (1 part sugar to 4 parts water). You can use a heavier syrup if you like: that's the joy of preserving – you control the sugar and flavours, so own it, ladies and gents! Combine the sugar with the water in a saucepan and heat it, stirring, until the sugar dissolves.

Sterilise your jars and lids before you begin by running them through the hottest cycle on the dishwasher or washing thoroughly, then drying them in a 180°C (350°F) oven for 15 minutes.

Next prepare your fruit. If I'm using stone fruit, I cut it in half, discard the stones and sometimes cut it into quarters – it's all very basic but the fruit needs to be in even-sized pieces. Pack the fruit as tightly as possible into your sterilised jars (use a wooden spoon to push the pieces down, but don't be rough and bruise the fruit). Pour in the sugar syrup, leaving about 1 cm (½ inch) of space at the top.

Slide a knife down and around the inside of each jar to release any air bubbles, then give the jar a good tap on the bench. Seal, then place in the preserving unit and follow the instructions. If you're using a stockpot or saucepan, pour in enough cold water to come at least three-quarters of the way up the sides of your jars, bring to the boil, then turn down and simmer on the lowest heat for 2 hours.

Remove the jars from the water using either tongs or a tea towel with great care and let them cool, then store in a dark corner of the kitchen.

FRUIT TO PRESERVE

~ **Apricots** with toasted cardamom pods

~ **Peaches** with ginger syrup (when making the sugar syrup, add 1 teaspoon grated ginger)

~ **Figs** with vanilla syrup (see page 43)

~ **Plums** with spiced syrup (when making the sugar syrup, add a cinnamon stick, star anise and some ground nutmeg)

STOCKPOT OR PRESERVING UNIT?

I have a great old Fowlers preserving unit that makes the whole process easy. You can source new and used kits online or from speciality shops. You'll also need to invest in Fowlers jars, lids, clips and rings. If you do go down this route, may I suggest joining the Facebook group 'Fowlers Vacola Users'? Once inside this treasure trove of knowledge, you can ask any preserving question and be the recipient of much generous and accurate advice. While a Fowlers unit does make bottling easier, a big stockpot or pan and clean glass jars and metal lids will also do the job. If going down this road, it's important to stop the jars from touching the bottom of the pan – place them on a small metal rack or a folded tea towel and then wrap each jar in a tea towel so they don't clang against each other and break.

FRUIT COBBLER

Delicious, simple and comforting – this cherry cobbler is my kind of baking. Basically a sponge topped with fruit, then baked and sprinkled with sugar, it's the sort of thing your gran might have served with Sunday lunch. It tastes honest and good, like proper puddings should. And it's a fabulous way to showcase your preserved fruit through the bare winter months. That said, it's also lovely made with fresh seasonal fruit at any time of the year. Thank you to Lesley Russell for sharing this recipe with me.

120 g (4^1/$_4$ oz) butter, softened, plus extra for greasing
^{1}/$_2$ cup (110 g) caster sugar, plus extra for sprinkling
2 eggs
1^2/$_3$ cups (250 g) self-raising flour
^{1}/$_3$ cup (80 ml) milk
2 cups (400 g) preserved cherries, apricots, plums or peaches

Preheat the oven to 180°C (350°F). Butter a shallow ovenproof dish.

Cream the butter and sugar together until light and fluffy. Add the eggs one at a time, beating well after each addition. Stir in the flour and milk to make a fairly stiff batter.

Spread the batter over the base of the dish. Arrange the fruit over the batter, leaving gaps here and there. Don't worry if a bit of juice comes with the fruit – it makes the cobbler more moist.

Bake in the centre of the oven for 30 minutes or until cooked through when tested with a skewer. As soon as you take the cobbler out of the oven, sprinkle it with extra sugar. Serve immediately, with cream or ice cream.

SERVES 6–8

OTHER THINGS TO MAKE WITH BOTTLED FRUIT

~ Blitz 1 cup (200 g) preserved apricots with ^{1}/$_2$ cup (125 ml) of the preserving liquid in a blender. Stir the purée through whipped cream and serve with crushed meringues (page 36) and amaretti biscuits for a fancy Eton mess.

~ Pour a jar of preserved stone fruit or figs into an ovenproof dish, cover with Crumble topping (page 75) and bake until golden and bubbling. Serve with ice cream and custard (page 75).

~ Gently warm bottled fruit to serve with porridge, cream and a sprinkle of Sweet dukkah (page 72) for a special winter breakfast.

~ Serve with plain yoghurt and a little granola.

~ Fold through a simple butter cake batter.

~ Add to smoothies.

~ Serve piled onto pancakes with plain yoghurt.

STONE FRUIT AND REDCURRANT CHUTNEY

This is absolutely delicious with warm ham and crusty bread, dolloped on a quiche or frittata, served with Pork and pistachio terrine (page 25), spread over a chunk of good cheddar cheese or spooned onto plates of barbecued short-loin lamb chops or sausages. In short: it's very useful and makes a great present.

If you're new to the world of preserving, this is a good place to start. Chutneys are much more forgiving than jam, there are far less rules and there's more room to improvise with ingredients. I've used apricots, but you can use any stone fruit: peaches, nectarines or plums would all be great. The redcurrants add a gorgeous pop of flavour and colour, but if they aren't available, just make up the weight with more stone fruit.

1 kg (2 lb 4 oz) stone fruit
2 brown onions, finely diced
1²/₃ cups (250 g) dried cranberries
1²/₃ cups (250 g) fresh or frozen redcurrants
2 cups (440 g) firmly packed soft brown sugar
6 cm (2¹/₂ inch) piece ginger, peeled and
    finely chopped
1 Tbsp sea salt
1 cinnamon stick
A good pinch of chilli flakes, or to taste
2 cups (500 ml) apple cider vinegar

Halve the stone fruit, discarding the stones, and cut into quarters.

Combine the fruit and all the remaining ingredients in a large heavy-based saucepan over medium–low heat. Cook for a few minutes until the sugar dissolves, then increase the heat to high and bring to the boil. Reduce the heat to medium–low and cook for about 45 minutes or until the chutney is glossy and thick. Transfer to sterilised jars to store.

MAKES ABOUT 3 JARS

RASPBERRY VINEGAR CORDIAL

This recipe comes via my husband's late father, Andrew. Andrew was a much-loved country vet and deer farmer (he began our journey with Mandagery Creek Venison some 30 years ago). He introduced me to this recipe, with memories of his grandmother making it for him as a boy. If you're lucky enough to have raspberries growing at home, do try this lovely and different way of preserving them.

I'd never tried raspberry vinegar cordial before Andrew suggested it and I was really pleasantly surprised. It's sweet and fruity, but balanced with the vinegar's acidity. It's very refreshing served over crushed ice with mineral water. You could throw in a splash of vodka if you're feeling festive.

500 g (1 lb 2 oz) raspberries
2 cups (500 ml) white wine vinegar
4 cups (880 g) sugar

Wash the raspberries, then drain and place in a large bowl. Add the vinegar and use a wooden spoon, pestle or the end of a rolling pin to bash the raspberries into the vinegar until you have a rough slush. Cover with a tea towel and set aside for a day for the raspberries and vinegar to get to know each other (don't put it in the fridge).

Strain the raspberry mixture through a fine sieve or muslin bag, extracting as much liquid as possible. The more force you use, the cloudier it will become – that doesn't bother me but if you want a clearer cordial, don't force the mixture through the sieve.

Transfer the raspberry liquid to a saucepan and bring to the boil, then add the sugar and whisk to combine. Boil for 5 minutes, then pour into sterilised bottles and immediately seal.

MAKES ABOUT 2 CUPS (500 ML)

If you're new to preserving, it's a good
idea to start with a chutney.

A tray of seasonal fruit always
makes a beautiful summertime gift.

Gift trays and baskets

Rosemary crackers and honey labna ~ Home-made crème fraîche and toasted cardamom sugar
Vanilla salt ~ Lime chilli salt ~ Cold vanilla and buttermilk soup ~ Chocolate sauce and sweet dukkah

One of my mum's dear friends, who recently finished breast cancer treatment,
told me she'd been blown away by the thoughtful care packages from friends and family.
The most wonderful discovery was a tray of fresh figs and a hunk of blue cheese on her
doorstep after coming home from chemo one summer afternoon. Another memorable
gift was a basket containing soft socks, magazines and boiled sweets, and the loan of
a beloved cashmere wrap. Small slices of comfort in and amongst all the
discomfort of that horrible illness.

Who wouldn't love a tray of fresh, seasonal fruit, accompanied by any of the following
delightful combinations? Minimal cooking, lots of flavour and such a good simple
present for anyone. Including yourself.

Rosemary crackers and honey labna with figs

Packaged up in a little pot with some crackers and fresh figs, honey labna is such a treat.

ROSEMARY CRACKERS
AND HONEY LABNA (WITH FIGS)

Rosemary crackers are beautiful with fresh figs and my honey labna, but also with dips or any soft white cheese. If you have a pasta machine then pull it out for this recipe – you can use a rolling pin but the crackers won't be quite as thin. Honey labna is best friends with all summer fruits.

Rosemary crackers

1 cup (150 g) plain flour, plus extra
  for dusting
A pinch of sugar
2 Tbsp rosemary, finely chopped
1/3 cup (80 ml) olive oil
2 Tbsp honey
Sea salt, for sprinkling

Honey labna

500 g (1 lb 2 oz) Greek-style
  yoghurt
2 Tbsp honey
1 tsp salt
1 vanilla bean, split lengthways

Rosemary crackers

Combine the flour, sugar, rosemary, olive oil and 1/4 cup (60 ml) water in a large bowl and mix well. Turn out onto a work surface and knead until you have a smooth dough, about 2–3 minutes. Cover with plastic wrap and leave to rest in the fridge for 30 minutes.

Preheat the oven to 180°C (350°F). Line three large baking trays with baking paper.

Divide the dough into three pieces. Take one piece of dough, leaving the rest covered with the plastic wrap so it doesn't dry out. Flatten the dough between your hands so you have a rough rectangle. Lightly dust it with flour, then feed it through the widest setting of a pasta machine. Repeat with the next setting, and again until you end up with a lovely long, thin sheet of dough. Cut the sheet in half and place it on one of the trays. Repeat with the remaining dough.

Combine the honey and 2 teaspoons water in a small saucepan and stir over medium heat until the honey dissolves into the water. Brush the mixture over the dough and sprinkle with sea salt.

Pop the trays into the oven and bake for 10–15 minutes or until the flatbread is thin and crunchy. Leave to cool, then break into crackers, ready to serve. Store in an airtight container.

MAKES ABOUT 20 SMALL CRACKERS OR 6 LONG CRACKERS

Honey labna

Place a sieve over a bowl. Line the sieve with a piece of muslin or a clean Chux cloth.

Put the yoghurt, honey and salt in a separate bowl. Scrape the seeds from the vanilla bean into the mixture, and stir until combined. Spoon into the sieve, gather the cloth into a loose ball and secure tightly with an elastic band. Pop the ball into the sieve over the bowl and refrigerate for 48 hours – the longer it's left, the thicker the labna will become.

MAKES ABOUT 1 CUP

HOME-MADE CRÈME FRAÎCHE
AND TOASTED CARDAMOM SUGAR (WITH PEACHES)

This is a perfect gift tray or afternoon treat when peaches are in season. Slice juicy, ripe peaches and dip into the tangy home-made crème fraîche, then sprinkle with the toasted cardamom sugar. Cardamom is my all-time favourite spice and when toasted and ground, its warm flavours are heightened to new levels of deliciousness, taking on an intense, almost warm minty aroma that is far more powerful than regular ground cardamom.

The toasted cardamom sugar is also lovely with pineapple, orange, apricot, pear, apple... I could go on. And on. For example, generously sprinkle the sugar over halved plums, dot with a little butter and roast until soft, then serve with vanilla ice cream. Or toast a really nice slice of fruit loaf, spread it with crème fraîche or ricotta and sprinkle it with cardamom sugar.

You might find it unrealistic to suggest you make crème fraîche rather than buy it. And of course, there's nothing stopping you from doing the latter. However, crème fraîche can be tricky to find for us country mice. Plus, making this otherwise expensive stuff at home is as easy as stirring a little cream and buttermilk together and leaving it on the bench for a day or two. This recipe makes a lovely thick, tangy version that will keep in the fridge for up to 2 weeks.

You can also dollop the tangy crème fraîche on fresh berries.

Ground toasted cardamom
1/3 cup (35 g) cardamom pods

Preheat the oven to 140°C (275°F). Scatter the cardamom pods over a baking tray and bake for 10 minutes or until beginning to turn dark green. Leave to cool, then transfer to a high-powered blender, food processor, spice grinder or coffee grinder and blitz as finely as possible. Pass the ground cardamom through a sieve to remove any larger pieces.

Store in an airtight container as the best ground cardamom ever, or use to make cardamom sugar.

MAKES ABOUT 1¹/2 TABLESPOONS

Toasted cardamom sugar
2 tsp ground toasted cardamom, or to taste
1/2 cup (110 g) golden caster sugar (or regular caster sugar)
A pinch of sea salt

Mix the ground toasted cardamom and sugar to taste and add the salt. Check the flavour – if it's too strong for you, add a little more sugar.

This mixture will stay potent in flavour for up to a week when stored in a jar out of direct sunlight.

MAKES ABOUT 1/2 CUP

Home-made crème fraîche
1 cup (250 ml) single (pure) cream
2 Tbsp buttermilk

Whisk the cream and buttermilk in a large jar. Place a layer of muslin or a clean Chux cloth on top and secure with twine or an elastic band, to stop bugs, dust or anything else getting into the mixture.

Leave the mixture to do its thing on the bench for 24 hours – it should thicken to the consistency of a good Greek-style yoghurt. If needed, leave it for another 24 hours. Stir well, transfer to a container with a lid and store in the fridge for up to 2 weeks.

MAKES ABOUT 1 CUP

VANILLA SALT
(WITH TOMATOES)

I discovered this wondrous condiment thanks to Renee Erickson's book, *A Boat, a Whale and a Walrus*. Her flavour combinations are a great source of inspiration to me and when she suggested making vanilla salt to sprinkle on tomatoes and poached fruits, I was smitten. A little jar of this stuff makes a great present to say thanks for having us for dinner, thanks for teaching my angel all year, and so on.

1 cup (225 g) sea salt flakes
2 vanilla beans, split lengthways

Place the sea salt in a small bowl. Scrape the vanilla seeds into the salt, and use your fingers to work them together. Divide the vanilla salt into small jars and add the empty vanilla beans (they'll keep imparting flavour). Serve with ripe tomatoes of any variety.

NOTE
For a super-delicious dessert, take another cue from Renee Erickson and serve vanilla ice cream with a sprinkle of vanilla salt and a drizzle of olive oil. (I know it sounds weird but it tastes amazing.) Make your own ice cream using the custard on page 75 and churn it in an ice cream machine, according to the manufacturer's instructions.

MAKES ABOUT 1 CUP

LIME CHILLI SALT
(WITH WATERMELON)

This chilli salt is wonderful with juicy watermelon as I've suggested here, as well as pan-fried fish, barbecued chicken or sliced peaches. It also makes a worthwhile hangover helper when sprinkled on peanut butter toast with an extra squeeze of lime!

Zest of 2 limes, peeled off in strips
1 bird's eye chilli, chopped
1 cup (225 g) sea salt flakes (pink if you can find them)

Preheat the oven to 140°C (275°F). Line a baking tray with baking paper. Put the lime zest on one half of the tray and chilli on the other. Cook for 20 minutes or until dried and beginning to curl up around the edges.

Using a spice grinder or mortar and pestle, finely chop or pound the lime zest, and then the chilli. Mix the lime zest and chilli with the sea salt and store in a jar.

MAKES ABOUT 1 CUP

COLD VANILLA
AND BUTTERMILK SOUP
(WITH RASPBERRIES)

This tangy chilled soup is a refreshing treat on a hot day. Packaged in a thermos with some fresh raspberries and Brunekager biscuits (page 45), it makes a beautiful gift.

2 egg yolks
$1/3$ cup (75 g) caster sugar
1 vanilla bean, split lengthways
4 cups (1 litre) buttermilk
Grated zest of 1 lemon

Beat the egg yolks and sugar together in a bowl until pale and frothy. Scrape the vanilla seeds into the yolk mixture. Add the buttermilk and lemon zest and whisk well. Cover the bowl and pop it in the fridge to chill for at least 3 hours.

MAKES ABOUT 4 CUPS

CHOCOLATE SAUCE AND SWEET DUKKAH
(WITH CHERRIES)

This dukkah is incredibly useful to have in the pantry and can jazz up pretty much anything with flavour and crunch. I sprinkle it on everything from porridge to Bircher muesli, cheesecakes, poached and fresh fruit, and pancakes with yoghurt. Here, with chocolate sauce and cherries, it makes a smart goodie box that anyone would be thrilled to find on their doorstep.

Chocolate sauce
1 cup (250 ml) single (pure) cream
1 1/3 cups (200 g) chopped good-
    quality dark chocolate
1 Tbsp (20 g) butter

Sweet dukkah
1/2 cup (75 g) hazelnuts or walnuts
1/3 cup (50 g) sesame seeds
2 Tbsp poppy seeds
1/2 tsp coriander seeds
2/3 cup (100 g) raw unsalted
    pistachio nuts
1/2 tsp ground cardamom
    (see page 68 for my ground
    toasted cardamom)
1/2 tsp ground cinnamon
1/4 tsp ground nutmeg
2 Tbsp soft brown sugar
A pinch of sea salt

Chocolate sauce
Heat the cream in a small saucepan over medium–high heat until just at boiling point. Remove from the heat and stir through the chocolate and butter until melted and smooth.

Store and seal in a jar or bottle in the fridge (it will need to sit at room temperature for an hour or so to soften up before serving).

MAKES ABOUT 1 1/2 CUPS

Sweet dukkah
Preheat the oven to 180°C (350°F). Spread the hazelnuts or walnuts on a baking tray and toast for 5 minutes. Add the sesame seeds, poppy seeds and coriander seeds and continue to toast for another 5 minutes. Remove from the oven.

Combine the hazelnuts or walnuts and pistachios in a food processor or use a mortar and pestle and blitz or bash until the mixture resembles coarse breadcrumbs. Add the toasted seeds, spices, brown sugar and salt. Give it another quick blitz or bash and mix to combine, then store in a jar or airtight container.

MAKES ABOUT 1 1/2 CUPS

ROUGH PUFF PASTRY

250 g (9 oz) chilled butter, cut into cubes
1²/₃ cups (250 g) plain flour, plus extra for dusting
¼ cup (60 ml) chilled water

Combine the butter and flour on the bench, using the heel of your hand to work them together. Add water as necessary to form a rough dough – it's okay to see some marbled streaks of butter. Cover with plastic wrap and chill in the fridge for 30 minutes.

On a lightly floured work surface, roll out the pastry until you have a large rectangle. Dust off any loose flour. Fold the top half of the pastry down, then fold the bottom half up so you have a long slim rectangle. Now turn the pastry 90 degrees and roll into another large rectangle, trying to roll in only one direction if possible (this helps keep the butter's 'marbled' effect and ideally will keep your pastry nice and puffy and flaky). Fold and roll again, then cover with plastic wrap and chill for 20 minutes or until needed.

MAKES ENOUGH FOR ONE LARGE TART

BASIC SWEET DOUGH

1 cup (250 ml) milk
100 g (3¹/₂ oz) butter
3 tsp dried yeast
¼ cup (55 g) caster sugar
1 egg
3¹/₃ cups (500 g) plain flour,
* plus extra for dusting*
A pinch of salt

Combine the milk and butter in a small saucepan. Heat, stirring, until the milk is warm and the butter has melted. Remove from the heat and set aside to cool until lukewarm.

Tip the milk and butter mixture into the bowl of an electric mixer with a dough attachment.

Add the yeast, sugar, egg, flour and salt and knead for 5 minutes. Turn out onto a lightly floured work surface and finish kneading by hand for a minute or so. (You can do the entire kneading process by hand – combine the dry ingredients on a work surface, make a well in the centre and then add the milk and butter mixture and egg, and knead everything together.)

Place the dough in a lightly oiled bowl, cover with a tea towel and leave in a warm place for 1 hour or until doubled in size.

MAKES ENOUGH FOR ONE LARGE TWISTED SWEET BUN OR ABOUT SIX INDIVIDUAL CINNAMON TWISTS (PAGE 46)

CUSTARD

1 1/4 cups (310 ml) milk
1 1/4 cups (310 ml) single (pure) cream
1 vanilla bean
1/3 cup (75 g) caster sugar
1 Tbsp cornflour
6 egg yolks

Combine the milk and cream in a saucepan over medium–high heat. Split the vanilla bean lengthways and scrape the seeds into the pan. Add the vanilla bean and heat until the mixture is almost boiling.

Whisk the sugar, cornflour and egg yolks until pale and creamy. Splash a little of the warm milk mixture into the egg yolk mixture and whisk again, then pour in the remaining milk mixture. Mix well, then return the whole lot to the saucepan. Stir over low heat for 5 minutes or until the custard is just about coating the back of your wooden spoon. Discard the vanilla bean, pour into a jug and store in the fridge until ready to serve.

MAKES ABOUT 3 CUPS

CRUMBLE TOPPING

280 g (10 oz) unsalted butter
2 cups (300 g) plain flour
1 cup (220 g) firmly packed soft brown sugar
1/4 tsp ground cinnamon
A pinch of salt
3/4 cup (115 g) toasted hazelnuts
1 1/3 cups (135 g) rolled oats

Preheat the oven to 180°C (350°F).

Combine the butter, flour, brown sugar, cinnamon, salt and hazelnuts in the bowl of a food processor and blitz for a few seconds, until just combined. (Or combine in a large bowl and work together with your fingertips until coarse and lumpy.) Add the oats and mix well. If you're freezing any of the crumble mixture, transfer it to a container or snap-lock bag now and then pop it into the freezer.

Spread the crumble mixture over a couple of baking trays and bake for 20 minutes or until just beginning to turn golden. Toss it around halfway through cooking so nothing gets stuck on the trays.

Sprinkle the roasted crumble mixture over warm poached fruit and bake for 20 minutes.

NOTE
This recipe makes more than you'll need for one crumble, and this is because I'd love you to set aside half the crumble mixture and pop it in the freezer. That means you are only ever a few unpeeled apples away from having a gorgeous crumble in the oven. You can also spread it over a baking tray and bake until crunchy, then use it as a rich granola-style topping for ice cream, roasted fruit, yoghurt and fresh fruit for breakfast, and so on.

MAKES ABOUT 4 CUPS

ACKNOWLEDGEMENTS

This book is for Tim, Alice and Tom. Our little family is everything to me. Thank you, guys, for your love and support, and, right back at you.

As anyone whose primary income depends on primary industry knows, the farming life can be really hard. It's a juggle, a gamble and a 24 hour/ 7 days a week job. And yes, it's a cliche, but despite the challenges we do look around us every day and feel grateful we get to live here on this farm, in this place together. Thank you, Tim and ALL of the farmers who grow and produce our food, for keeping the boat afloat through drought, bushfires, all the uncertainties and challenges.

Thank you to my parents, Annie and Henry Herron, whose beautiful property features prominently throughout this book. Thank you for giving my siblings and me confidence, opportunity and a home we always love to come back to.

Thank you to the team at Murdoch Books, especially Corinne Roberts who has guided me through this process with such skill and warmth, and designer Vivien Valk who has worked so hard to make this book so beautiful.

Big thanks to Josie Chapman for opening up her beautiful cottages at the Old Convent B&B Borenore for some of the photography.

Making and sharing good, simple, seasonal food is an act of love and generosity, so my final thanks is to you, for buying this book and hopefully taking inspiration from it to go out and leave a basket of home-made food at someone's door soon. It will mean so much to them.

INDEX

This edition published in 2020 by Murdoch Books, an imprint of Allen & Unwin
Content originally published in *A Basket by the Door*, published in 2019 by Murdoch Books

Murdoch Books UK
Ormond House, 26–27 Boswell Street,
London, WC1N 3JZ
Phone: +44 (0) 20 8785 5995
murdochbooks.co.uk
info@murdochbooks.co.uk

For corporate orders & custom publishing contact our business development team at salesenquiries@murdochbooks.com.au

Publisher: Corinne Roberts
Cover design: northwoodgreen.com
Internal design: Vivien Valk
Editor: Justine Harding
Production director: Lou Playfair

Photography: Sophie Hansen, except page 2 by Clancy Paine

ISBN 978 1 911 63280 1

A catalogue record for this book is available from the British Library

Printed by C&C Offset Printing Co Ltd, China

TABLESPOONS: We have used Australian 20 ml (4 teaspoon) tablespoon measures. If you are using a smaller European 15 ml (3 teaspoon) tablespoon, add an extra teaspoon of the ingredient for each tablespoon specified in the recipe.

10 9 8 7 6 5 4 3 2 1